$\mathcal{P}$resented to:

_____

$\mathcal{B}$y:

_____

Perfect Trust

Ears to Hear, Hearts to Trust,
and Minds to Rest in Him

CHARLES R. SWINDOLL

THOMAS NELSON
Since 1798

NASHVILLE   DALLAS   MEXICO CITY   RIO DE JANEIRO

Published in Nashville, Tennessee, by Thomas Nelson®. Thomas Nelson is a registered trademark of Thomas Nelson, Inc.

Thomas Nelson, Inc., titles may be purchased in bulk for educational, business, fund-raising, or sales promotional use. For information, please e-mail SpecialMarkets@ThomasNelson.com.

ISBN: 978-1-4003-2010-3

Printed in China

12 13 14 15 [RRD] 4 3 2

www.thomasnelson.com

Contents

Preface

We take a look at the money in our pockets and it says, "In God we trust." Trust Him to do what? Keep us free from invasion? Make us prosperous? Sustain our position of world power and leadership? Revolutionary War soldiers used to say, "Trust in God but keep your powder dry." Yet as a nation today we are much more self-reliant (keeping our powder dry) than we are God-reliant (trusting in Him).

Here's a direct question: "Can you trust God?" There are two ways to look at that question. "Can you *trust* God?" That is, is He dependable in times of need? Will He do what He says? Or, secondly, we might ask, "Can *you* trust God?" Do *you* have such a relationship with Him and such confidence in Him that you believe He is with you always even though you do not see any evidence of His presence and His power?

It isn't easy to trust God in times of adversity. Feelings of distress, despair, and darkness trouble our souls as we wonder if God truly cares about our plight. But *not to trust* Him is to doubt His sovereignty and to question His goodness. In order to trust God we must view our adverse circumstances through eyes of faith, not our senses. And just as the faith of salvation comes through hearing the message of the gospel (Romans 10:17), so the faith to trust God in adversity comes through the Word of God alone. It is only in the Scriptures that we find an adequate view of God's relationship to and involvement in our painful circumstances. It is only through Scripture, applied to our hearts by the Holy Spirit, that we receive the grace to trust God in everything.

That is why I have made Scripture the basis of this book. My hope is that by examining the characteristics of God and reviewing His trustworthiness in the lives of ordinary men and women, we will be inspired to trust Him more fully ourselves. I want you to find rest from the weariness of worry and the plagues of doubt and fear. I want us to be a distinctive people—people who step out in faith even when the future is fuzzy, people whose lives reflect a quiet peace and calm assurance because we have cultivated perfect trust in God.

That kind of trust frees us to become the distinctive people God is calling us to be. The kind of Christian A. W. Tozer describes like this:

He feels supreme love for
One he's never seen.
He talks familiarly every day to
Someone he cannot see.
He expects to go to heaven on
the virtue of Another.

He empties himself in order to be full.

He admits he is wrong so he

can be declared right.

He goes down in order to get up.

He is strongest when he is weakest,

richest when he is poorest,

happiest when he feels the worst.

He dies so he can live.

He forsakes in order to have.

He gives away so he can keep.

He sees the invisible.

He hears the inaudible.

He knows that which passes understanding.[1]

My prayer is that this little book will help you to

trust God not only in the pit of dire circumstances

but also on the pinnacle of abundance and success.

Chuck Swindoll
January 2000

God is never at a loss to know what He's going to do in our situations. He knows perfectly well what is best for us. Our problem is, *we* don't know.

$\mathcal{T}$here is no impossible situation that God cannot handle. He won't handle it necessarily your way, but He'll handle it.

Give Me a
Heart to Trust

Give Me a
Heart to Trust

I can't think of anyone more suitable to inspire our trust in God than the psalmist David. He was hunted, haunted, and hounded by his enemies even though God had promised him a future of leadership. He was the anointed king-elect, but Saul was still on the throne. David inspires us because we read of his trust in God during those years of relentless adversity. In Psalm 4:3 he said, "Know that the LORD has set apart the godly man for Himself; the LORD hears when I call to Him." He was so sure of God that he later added, "In peace I will both lie down and sleep, for You alone, O LORD, make me to dwell in safety" (v. 8).

When the Philistines seized David in Gath, he said, "When I am afraid, I will put my trust in You.

In God, whose word I praise, in God I have put my trust; I shall not be afraid. What can mere man do to me?" (Psalm 56:3–4). When he fled from Saul into a cave, David cried out to God: "Be gracious to me, O God, be gracious to me, for my soul takes refuge in You; and in the shadow of Your wings I will take refuge until destruction passes by" (Psalm 57:1).

Many, many years ago, Felix of Nola was escaping his enemies, and he, too, took temporary refuge in a cave. He had scarcely entered the opening of the cave before a spider began to weave its web across the small opening. With remarkable speed, the insect completely sealed off the mouth of the cave with an intricate web, giving the appearance that the cave had not been entered for many weeks. As Felix's pursuers passed by, they saw the web and didn't even bother to look inside. Later, as the godly fugitive stepped out into the sunlight, he uttered these insightful words: "Where God is, a spider's web is a wall; where He is not, a wall is but a spider's web."

Along the path of life, we also find ourselves in cave-like struggles. Sometimes the things we go through are our own fault. We deserve judgment instead of relief. At other times we are caught in a dark place because of what others have done or as a result of circumstances beyond our control. Regardless of the cause of our "cave," we can pray with David, "Let me hear Your lovingkindness in the morning; for I trust in You; teach me the way in which I should walk; for to You I lift up my soul" (Psalm 143:8). David wanted God's will to be accomplished in his life. He trusted God to show him the way through the difficulties—up and over the rugged rocks to a smooth highway.

Strength

But what about those times when we trust in God yet disaster strikes? We are tempted to doubt and question, "Why?" We ask, "God, if You are my safety, why am I in this situation?"

Helen Roseveare was a British medical missionary in the Congo years ago during an uprising. Her faith was strong and her trust was confident, yet she was raped and assaulted and treated brutally. Commenting later, she said, "I must ask myself a question as if it came directly from the Lord: 'Can you thank Me for trusting you with this experience even if I never tell you why?'"

Worry drains our energy and makes us tired, because prior to the actual battle, we fight the Enemy

a hundred times in our minds . . .
Relax. Untie those knots of anxiety with the settled assurance that
the Holy Spirit will be there in
your moment of need.

What a profound thought. God has trusted each
of us with our own set of unfair circumstances and
unexplained experiences to deal with. Can we still
trust Him even if He never tells us why?

The secret to responsible trust is *acceptance*.
Acceptance is taking from God's hand absolutely
anything He gives, looking into His face in trust
and thanksgiving, knowing that the confinement
of the hedge we're in is good and for His glory.
Even though what we're enduring may be painful, it's good simply because God Himself has
allowed it. Acceptance is resting in God's goodness, believing that He has all things under His

control—even people who are doing what is wrong. Yes, even wrongdoers.

Christianity is trusting Christ, not self. Most people are trying to reach God, find God, and please God through their own efforts. But perfect trust is resting all of one's weight on something else, not on self. It's like resting on crutches to hold you up when you twist an ankle. You lean on them as your strength. Proverbs 3:5–6 teaches us to "trust in the LORD with all your heart and do not lean on your own understanding. In all your ways acknowledge Him, and He will make your paths straight." In other words, strength comes from proper perspective. Elton Trueblood put it this way: "Faith is not belief without proof, but trust without reservation." Strength comes from choosing to fully trust, pray, and praise. Our circumstances may not change, but in the process, we change.

This is how Andrew Murray stated it:

First, He brought me here, it is by His will I am in this straight place: in that fact I will rest.

Next, He will keep me here in His love, and give me the grace to behave as His child.

Then, He will make the trial a blessing, teaching me lessons He intends for me to learn, and working in me the grace He means to bestow.

Last, in His good time, He can bring me out again—how and when, He knows.[2]

Serenity

Serenity is another word for peace, something we all long to have. But this peace isn't a nirvana hypnotic trance or something encountered by repeating a mantra a thousand times.

It isn't acquired through yoga exercises or crystals or channeling or counsel from a guru in Tibet. Where do we find this peace? Peace comes from trusting in God. "The steadfast of mind You will keep in perfect peace, because he trusts in You" (Isaiah 26:3). It comes from dwelling in the shelter and finding refuge in the shadow of the Almighty (Psalm 91:1–2).

In his letter to the Roman Christians, Paul recounted a litany of the effects of God's goodness toward us: we are forgiven, strengthened by His Spirit, and granted wisdom, sonship, and hope. We are promised the prayers of Christ for our needs and the certainty of an eternal destiny and purpose. Following all this, Paul paused and asked, "What then shall we say to these things? If God is for us, who is against us? He who did not spare His own Son, but delivered Him over for us all, how will He not also with Him freely give us all things?" (Romans 8:31–32).

We continually encounter hardships. People disappoint us. We disappoint ourselves. But God is constant and compassionate. We are not alone. He cares. Against all reason, the transcendent God loves us so much that He has committed Himself to us. That's why Paul could proclaim, "But in all these things we overwhelmingly conquer through Him who loved us. For I am convinced that neither death, nor life, nor angels, nor principalities, nor things present, nor things to come, nor powers, nor height, nor depth, nor any other created thing, will be able to separate us from the love of God, which is in Christ Jesus our Lord" (Romans 8:37–39).

God has entrusted a great deal to us. He knows that we can do all things by His grace, so He's trusting in us to trust in Him. Yet He knows our fears as well. Otherwise He wouldn't assure us so often of His purposes and His presence.

The secret to responsible trust is *acceptance*.

- We feel hurt and alone—God assures us He cares.
- We feel angry and resentful—God provides wisdom and strength.
- We feel ashamed—God promises to supply all our needs.

May He give us ears to hear, hearts to trust, and minds to rest in Him. Our God is uniquely and ultimately trustworthy!

Entrust. What a wonderful word! It is a banking term . . . meaning "to deposit." When it comes to trials, we deposit ourselves into God's safekeeping until that deposit yields eternal dividends.

When you deposit money in the bank, there's a limit on how much the FDIC will insure under one account ownership; usually it's about $100,000. But our infinite God has no limits. Millions upon multimillions of Christians can deposit themselves in His care, and He will make every one of them good. He will hold every one of us securely.

Trust When
You're Troubled

Trust When You're Troubled

We are all faced with a series of great opportunities, brilliantly disguised as unsolvable problems. Unsolvable without God's wisdom, that is. With His wisdom, they are changed to great opportunities. That change depends on our perspective. We are faced with a problem that seems to have no human solution. And perhaps it doesn't. There is no end in view. It has all the marks of an endlessly impossible situation. But I have found in my few years on earth that this is the platform upon which God does His greatest work. The more impossible the situation, the greater God accomplishes His work.

This truth is no better illustrated than in the life of Job, a man who went through great times of suffering until God finally brought rest and restoration. When I read the account of Job's plight, I cannot imagine it. He lost everything he owned—his home, all ten of his children, and his health. It is probably safe to say that not one of us has ever entered into such depths of misery and calamity. Remarkably, his first response to God was the response of worship: "Job arose and tore his robe and shaved his head, and he fell to the ground and worshiped" (Job 1:20).

You might expect him to fall to the ground and cry for mercy or to rant and rave that these back-to-back events were simply not fair. But he didn't. He worshiped. And not because he understood what was happening to him, but in spite of all that was happening to him. Not only did Job worship, he accepted what God had sent into his life. That is wisdom. That is perfect trust.

How was Job able to respond like this? First of all, he looked up and was comforted by God's sovereignty. When he *looked up* he saw a God who gave and took away. More than that, he saw the heart of God. He saw the sovereign love of God. Second, Job *looked ahead* and was reminded of God's promise that at the end it would all be made right. That spurred him on. Third, he *looked within* and saw that God had instructed him in his suffering and illness as in no other way. Like a piece of clay, Job willingly placed himself in the hands of the Master Potter. In essence Job said, "Do with me as You please. I trust You."

Job's response was rare then . . . and it's rare today. Trust is usually lacking when unsolvable problems emerge. When I think of a lack of trust, my mind goes back to the spies who went into the land of Canaan (Numbers 13). God had promised to give the land to His people. But the spies forgot all about the promise. The voice of God was suddenly silent because the lens of fear magnified the size of their uncertainty. They forgot all about the fruit of the land. They forgot all about God's power. They focused directly and only on the size of the enemy and the strength of the cities, even though there wasn't one city or entire tribe of the enemy greater than God.

It's the nature of the beast within us to keep going back to the familiar rather than to strap on faith and face the future. We are intimidated by the adventure, the excitement, and the delight of watching God block out the "giants" in the land. We want the safety of yesterday even though we know it's not where God would have us. Anything to avoid the uncertainties waiting around the bend – those unfamiliar surprises, unwanted fears, and unpleasant adversities.

Not only did Job worship, he accepted what God had sent into his life. That is wisdom. That is perfect trust.

But when God is in your circumstances and you come to a dangerous place, He magnificently delivers. He delivers wisdom right when you need it. He delivers protection. He delivers relief from discouragement and internal fortification from attack. If you run away, you nullify faith. You panic and cut God short. You short-circuit His opportunity to do what man cannot do. Stand firm! Believe Him! Give Him an opportunity to bring those afternoon miracles. Just before nightfall, He'll come through.

God is not known for doing standard things. He is engaged in doing very distinct things. When a person does something, it has the man or woman look about it. It drips with humanity. You can follow the logic of it and see the meaning behind it. You can even read what they paid for it and how they pulled it off and the organization that made it so slick. God doesn't build skyscrapers; men build skyscrapers. And they all have the touch of genius. Human genius. But you cannot find a man who can make a star. And when God steps in, His working is like the difference between a skyscraper and a star.

A classic example comes to mind. It happened back in the days of Daniel. His three Jewish friends, Shadrach, Meshach, and Abed-nego, refused to bow before a golden image of the king. Rather than worship that gigantic idol, they chose to trust their God to deliver them from the fiery furnace into which they were thrown. A humanly impossible situation? Absolutely.

God honored their convictions. He miraculously delivered them from the white-hot furnace. So amazed was the king, he extolled their God! In fact, he announced, "Blessed be the God of Shadrach, Meshach and Abed-nego, who has sent His angel and delivered His servants who *put their trust in Him*" (Daniel 3:28, italics mine).

Perfect trust resulted in divine deliverance.

We just take life one day at a time. That's the way God dispenses life. Because He never changes and He knows what will work together for our good and His glory. You and I don't.

Ever have something begin to kind of nag you? You can't put your finger on it. It's fuzzy. Sort of a slimy ooze. It's just growing in the corner, nagging you, getting you down. That is the beginning of a heavy anxiety. We need discernment to detect it, identify it, and get to its root, so we can deal with it. When we see the beginning of anxiety for what it is, that's the precise moment to cast it on God, to roll that pack on Him.

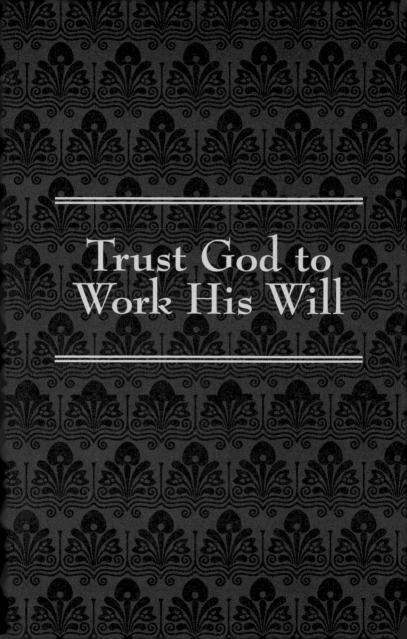

Trust God to
Work His Will

Trust God to
Work His Will

You know what? God personally cares about the things that worry us. He cares more about them than we care about them: those things that hang in our minds as nagging, aching, worrisome thoughts. First Peter 5:7 invites you to cast "all your anxiety on Him, because He cares for you." He cares. You are His personal concern. He cares about those aching thoughts that are like heavy anchors dragging you down.

Moses had an anchor dragging him down. Do you remember why he left Egypt when he was forty years old? He was running for his life. Pharaoh and some of his men were looking for Moses, to kill him (Exodus 2:15). Then forty years later God told Moses to return to Egypt (Exodus 3 and 4). Naturally Moses was worried about those men back in Egypt who wanted his head. He was reluctant to go back. But once he acquiesced to God's will, he said, "Lord, I'm available. I'm going to trust in You with all my heart. I'm not going to lean on my own understanding." Then while he was still in Midian, God said to him, "Oh, by the way Moses, you know all those men who sought your life? They're dead." Isn't that remarkable? What a tremendous relief for the old fellow!

His experience demonstrates the truth of Proverbs 3:5–6, which I call a before-and-after proverb. Certain things are to take place beforehand, which are our responsibility, so that afterward something might occur that is God's responsibility.

Let me explain. What is the *before* part? "Trust in the LORD with all your heart." That suggests relying on Him, letting Him take the lead, have first place, take over the controls . . . the steering wheel of our lives. We're to release all that to Him with *all* our hearts. This is not to be done halfheartedly, but without reservation. At this point Solomon added a warning: "Do not lean on your own understanding," which means, don't bring in the crutches and lean on them, those crutches that you have designed and made to handle such situations. Stay away from them. Don't lean on them; lean on God.

After the warning we are given the final part of the *before process*: "In all your ways acknowledge him." That word *acknowledge* in Hebrew could mean "to recognize." We are to recognize God, to remind ourselves that He is in charge.

Now the *after part*: "He will make your paths straight." That word *straight* means "smooth." God will smooth out your path. He'll take away the obstacles. He'll take care of those barriers when you come to them. If you'll do your part—give Him the steering wheel and trust Him to be in charge—He promises to make the path smooth.

That ties in with Proverbs 16:7, a twin proverb that fits these two verses perfectly: "When a man's ways are pleasing to the LORD, He makes even his enemies to be at peace with him." What a great promise! When your path is smooth and you are walking in obedience, God will ultimately make even your enemies be at peace with you. That means the barriers will come down. The impossible will become possible.

I don't have to explain or defend the will of God. My job is simply to obey it.

But let me caution you. This does not mean things will always turn out in your favor. You won't always get the car you dreamed of. You won't always get the degree at the time you planned it or the raise you anticipated or the promotion you hoped for. You won't always hold the job. We're not talking about a bargaining tool that you can use to manipulate God. We're talking about trust—perfect trust—that says, "Lord, I'm not going to worry and fret, day after day, hour after hour, about this whole process. It belongs to You. I give it to You. And I'm going to walk in obedience, as best I understand it, before Your Word, in keeping with Your will. I'm going to do it all Your way."

God takes care of the barriers when we take our hands off . . . and He often does it in the most surprising ways. As you walk the path of trust, you will experience situations that simply defy explanation. When you look back, after the fact, you realize you could never have figured out a better plan. At the time it seemed strange, mysterious . . . even illogical. Let me assure you, that's God working. Things will happen that seem to be totally contradictory, but these are God's arrangements. It was a wonderful day when I finally realized I don't have to explain or defend the will of God. My job is simply to obey it.

It is a waste of time trying to unscrew the inscrutable workings of God. You'll never be able to do it. That's simply the way God works. He honors faith and obedience. He will honor your faith if you will trust Him in a walk of obedience. And when you trust Him completely, you will enjoy inner quietness and security. You will have a secure confidence that you are walking in His will. You will be surrounded by His peace.

Leaving the details of
my future in God's hands
is the most responsible act
of obedience I can do.

Our sovereign Lord operates from an eternal agenda, not a daily planner. Sometimes, when we expect Him to charge over the hill with the cavalry, He holds back. Other times, at the exact moment we think He has misplaced our address, He comes in through the back door. And when we wonder if we'll ever feel His warmth, He pulls us in from the cold and sets us in front of His crackling fire . . . Even with all He has revealed about Himself in His Word, His hand often moves in ways we can't explain.

Why Let
Worry Wear
You Down?

Why Let Worry
Wear You Down?

In the depths of every person's soul, in the secret chambers where no one else knows the thoughts, we are usually able to find a worry or two or three. Even in the hearts of those who are laughing and smiling.

We worry about death—our own or that of a loved one. We worry about disobedience and sin, about feelings of guilt. We worry about daily problems—people problems, decision problems, problems related to work, home, relationships, finances, school . . . you name it, we worry about it.

Maybe you have a worry related to some simple, daily problem that eats away at your peace, like a rat in the corner of your life. It just gnaws and gnaws and gnaws. You can't seem to get out from under it. Maybe it was a foolish mistake you made and you're paying for it.

Jesus spoke about being worried or anxious in His Sermon on the Mount (Matthew 6 RSV). In fact He mentions this word six times in ten verses: "Do not be *anxious*" (25); "which of you by being *anxious*" (27); "Why are you *anxious* about clothing" (28); "do not be *anxious*" (31); and "do not be *anxious* about tomorrow; for tomorrow will be *anxious* for itself" (34).

Anxious. Intriguing word. It literally means "to be divided" or "distracted." It conveys the idea of being so mentally ill at ease that you cannot do what you need to do because you are so distracted in your thinking. That gnawing thought is pulling your mind toward it so you can't give yourself to the thing you need to do.

We find a perfect illustration of this in the story of Mary and Martha recorded in Luke 10:38–42.

Taking a minute to look into their little abode, we find that Martha is distracted, *anxious*. Jesus is sitting down talking, and Mary is sitting at His feet, enjoying His presence, His influence, and His teaching. But not Martha. She is busy back in the kitchen getting everything ready for a big meal. In good womanly fashion she is making everything match, everything fit, everything come out of the oven at just the right time, every dish prepared so it looks right and tastes good and is just tender enough but not overdone, and on and on and on. Unlike Mary, Martha is distracted.

But Jesus wanted her to come and sit down beside her sister and listen. It wasn't that He didn't appreciate her efforts. He just wanted her to serve a simple dish so they could make the most of their time together. Christ finally pointed out to her that her anxiety was distracting her from more important things. Worry always does that.

Five Problems with Worry

O ne of the problems with worry is that *it keeps you from enjoying what you have.* When you worry about what you don't have, you won't be able to enjoy what you do have. That's what Jesus was talking about in Matthew 6:25: "I tell you, do not be anxious about your life, as to what you shall eat or what you shall drink" (ESV). Worry is assuming responsibilities that you cannot handle.

I gird myself today with the power of God:

> God's strength to comfort me,
>
> God's might to uphold me,
>
> God's wisdom to guide me,
>
> God's eye to look before me,
>
> God's ear to hear me,
>
> God's word to speak for me,
>
> God's hand to lead me,

God's way to lie before me,

God's shield to protect me. . . .

ST. PATRICK'S BREASTPLATE

The truth is, they are responsibilities that God never intended for you to handle, because they are His.

Another problem with worry is that *it makes you forget your worth*. Worry makes you feel worthless, forgotten, and unimportant. That's why Jesus said that we are worth much more than the birds of the air who neither worry nor die of hunger because their heavenly Father feeds them (Matthew 6:26). They enjoy what's there. If God is able to sustain the lesser creatures, won't He sustain the greater? Maybe you're worried about things that seem important in your life. Yet your heavenly Father knows what is essential better than you do. And you are worth so much that He is taking things one at a time, dealing with more important things in your life right now.

There's a third argument against worry: *It is a complete waste of energy.* It solves nothing. That's why Jesus said, "Which of you by being anxious can add one cubit to his span of life?" (Matthew 6:27 RSV) In essence He was saying, "You go to bed tonight and fret and fuss because you're not five feet, eleven inches; you're only five feet, nine inches. But when you wake up in the morning, you're still going to be five feet, nine inches." Worry will never make you stretch! And it won't solve that anxiety on your mind either.

Let me be completely candid here. Do you know why we worry? We have a quiet, hidden *love* for worry! We enjoy it! When one worry is gone, we replace it with another. There's always a line of worries waiting to get in the door. So as one goes out the back door, we usher in the next one through the front door. We enjoy entertaining them. Worries are our mental and emotional companions. But Jesus said, in effect, that they're worthless!

The fourth problem with worry is that *it erases the promises of God from your mind.* Jesus implied this when He said, "O men of little faith: Therefore do not be anxious, saying, 'What shall we eat?' or 'What shall we drink?' or 'What shall we wear?'" (Matthew 6:31 RSV). The promise of God is that He will not allow His children to beg for bread. He will care for our needs, and that's the promise you can claim. Since He took care of our greatest need at Calvary by giving us Christ, then you can be sure He will take care of everything else He considers important for us.

This means encouragement if you are in school and beginning to feel overwhelmed with your studies. It's encouragement if you are busily engaged in raising a small family. It's encouragement if your family is almost gone or perhaps gone already and now you're alone, perhaps without a mate, and inclined to worry, "What will I do now?" But the worry erases from your mind the promise that God cares! He understands! He will take care of you!

The fifth problem is that *worry is characteristic of the heathen, not the Christian.* The man on the street who doesn't know the Lord, who doesn't have God personally involved in his life, is characterized by worry. It fits him. Who else can he lean on? But Christians have a heavenly Father who "knows that [they] need all these things" (Matthew 6:32). And if He knows that we have these needs and He considers these needs essential, He is not going to leave us alone with those needs unmet.

What to Do with Worry

Here's a question worth your time: What are we to do when worry comes knocking on the door of our minds? First, we must set our minds on Christ: "Seek first His king-dom and His righteousness, and all these things [that would worry you] will be added to you" (Matthew 6:33). When the temptation to worry first arrives, that's the critical moment. The tendency is to enter-tain it. To let it onto the front porch and allow it to sit there. But before you know it, worry has crawled in through the window and made itself at home! No! Worry must be stopped. We have to decide that we are going to commit this worry to God right now and refuse to entertain it, even on the front porch of our thinking.

Second, we must decide to live one day at a time. And that day is today . . . only *today*. I like what Robert Burdette wrote: "There are two days in the week about which I never worry. Two carefree days, kept sacredly free from fear and apprehension. One of these days is yesterday, and the other day I do not worry about is tomorrow."

When you worry about what you don't have, you won't be able to enjoy what you do have.

The third way to handle worry is explained by four simple words:

PRESENCE—Claim God's presence. Say to yourself "I'm not alone."

PROMISES—Recount God's promises. There are more than seven thousand of them in the Scriptures.

PRAYER—Tell God about your worry. After doing so, leave it with Him.

PATIENCE—Wait on God. Rather than rushing in and messing things up, trust His provision.

$\mathcal{D}$on't contaminate today by corrupting it with tomorrow's troubles. Refuse—yes, *refuse*— to allow tomorrow's lagoon of worries to drain into today's lake. Today is challenge enough!

When you face an impossibility, leave it in the hands of the Specialist. The things which are impossible with men are possible with God (Luke 18:27). Our problem is that we hold on to our problems.

Trust God for the Impossible

Trust God for the Impossible

Walking with God is the most exciting and rewarding of all experiences on earth. I should add, it is also the most difficult. I don't think I've ever met an exception to the rule, that those who walk closest to God are those who, like Jesus, become acquainted with trials and testings. God takes us through struggles and difficulties so that we might become increasingly more committed to Him.

That was never more true than in the life of Elijah. He was sitting beside the dried-up brook Cherith when God came to him and instructed him to go to a town called Zarephath, a word that means "to smelt or melt." Apparently, there was a smelting plant of some kind near this town, and that was the place God had designed for Elijah. He had been tested by the dried-up brook, and now came another time of testing. Zarephath was about one hundred miles from Cherith. That was a long walk, and it was across wilderness. At that time, Elijah was a wanted man—Ahab was pursuing him. Yet God told him to leave his place of security, a hidden place, and go to a place that was better known. It was a risk. He had to trust God on that long journey.

God also told Elijah that a widow would provide for him in the town. That was a humbling piece of information for the prophet. He wouldn't have minded if God had commanded *him* to provide for the widow. But no, God was going to have a *widow* provide for him. But God knew best and had prepared the woman for his arrival.

So Elijah obeyed God and made the lengthy journey to Zarephath. But when he arrived, there was nothing but a woman looking for sticks to build a fire to fix her last meal and die of starvation. From a human perspective the situation looked impossible. But what did Elijah do? He wasn't going to let the initial impression of an impossibility get him down. He rolled up the sleeves of his robe and said to the widow, "Do not fear; go, do as you have said, but make me a little bread cake from it first and bring it out to me, and afterward you may make one for yourself and for your son" (1 Kings 17:13).

> Since He took care of our greatest need at Calvary by giving us Christ, then you can be sure He will take care of everything else He considers important for us.

How did Elijah have the courage to talk like that? Stop and think. He had walked with God and had proven God faithful. You can't talk like that if you've never walked like that. You can't encourage somebody else to believe the impossible if you haven't believed the impossible yourself. Faith is like lighting the torch that passes from one person to the next. You can't light the torch of another if yours isn't burning. Elijah had been a hundred miles through a miracle. So when he met a widow with an empty oil bottle and an empty flour barrel, he could say, "That's no problem with God" Quiet trust prompts courage.

Have you ever been around a person of faith? Ever rubbed shoulders with men and women of God who didn't have the word *impossible* in their vocabulary? It's the most incredible association you can imagine. It's remarkable how it builds courage into your faith!

It certainly built the widow's faith. Especially when Elijah assured her with a promise of God's provision: "The bowl of flour shall not be exhausted, nor shall the jar of oil be empty, until the day that the LORD sends rain on the face of the earth" (1 Kings 17:14). What a promise! The woman looked at Elijah, a stranger who was covered with the dust and grime of a long journey, and she heard words like she had never heard before. Though she didn't know him, she listened to him . . . she believed him.

The most exciting part of this story is not the widow's willingness but God's faithfulness. When the woman obeyed God's instructions, God honored her obedience with two miracles: the bowl of flour was never empty; the jar of oil never ran dry.

God takes us through struggles and difficulties so that we might become increasingly more committed to Him.

How thrilling it must have been for that woman and her son and the prophet, who was now a part of the household, to sit down at the table and look at one miracle after another and eat them. Now, it doesn't mean they had everything they wanted. It means they had all they *needed*. Always remember, when you don't get what you want but God gives you what you need, that is the height of happiness. When God says no to your wants but yes to your needs, you are wonderfully content.

God may be leading you somewhere such as Zarephath, somewhere that doesn't make much sense. I want to encourage you: don't try to make sense out of it; just go. If God leads you to stay in a difficult situation and you have peace that you are to stay, don't analyze it; stay. Do your part. Do what He tells you to do, for His promises often hinge on obedience. God told Elijah to get up and go, so he got up and went. God told the widow to fix the meal, and she went and fixed it. They did their part, and God did His part—and they never ran out of food.

That doesn't mean they had a banquet; they had simple, little bread cakes morning, noon, and night. But they had food. Often, God's provisions are just enough, but don't fail to thank Him and to trust Him. Maybe you don't have the job you wanted. Maybe you don't have the position you planned. But His provisions are just enough and just right for this time.

You can walk with Him in perfect trust. That's your part.

God sees our need to trust
Him, and His love is so great
that He will not let us live
another day without turning
over our fears, our worries,
our confusion, so that nothing
becomes more significant
to us than our Father.

Trust in the LORD with all your heart and lean not on your own understanding; in all your ways acknowledge him, and he will make your paths straight.

PROVERBS 3:5–6 NIV

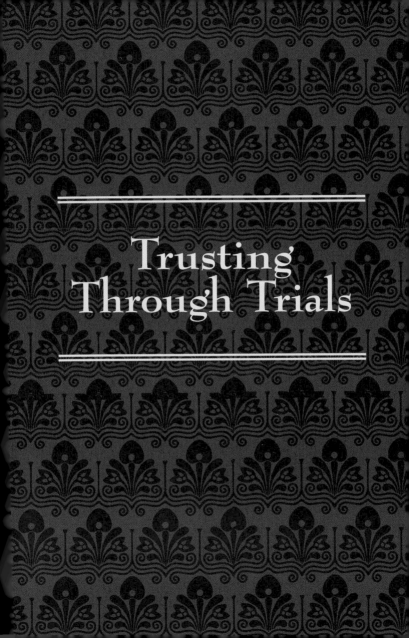

Trusting
Through Trials

Trusting Through Trials

It's impossible to pass through life without experiencing times when you cannot see your way through a deep valley. Times when the package delivered at the back door comes delivered in the ugly wrapping of death or affliction or illness or even divorce. Job was right when he wrote, "Man is born for trouble, as sparks fly upward" (Job 5:7). John Selden, the old British jurist and scholar, put it even more bluntly: "Pleasure is nothing else but intermission of pain."

You may find yourself enjoying the intermission. Today, you may be smiling. Your heart may be light and merry. Perhaps answers to prayer have come beautifully and deliberately. You are swept away in delight. But it's also quite possible that you are caught in the grip of affliction. You may be going through some of the hardest days of your life. You may be wondering, *Why? Why me? Why this trial?*

James wrote to Christians who were enduring great persecution. They were probably asking those same questions. He answered them in this way: "Blessed is a man who perseveres under trial; for once he has been approved, he will receive the crown of life which the Lord has promised to those who love Him" (James 1:12). He was saying that when you persevere through a trial, God gives you a special measure of insight. You become the recipient of the favor of God as He gives to you—and to those who suffer with you—something that would not be learned otherwise.

That word *persevere* is very important. It's an archaic word, and we don't hear much about it in our day of bailing out and giving up. We don't hear much about hanging in there and persevering . . . about staying power! But there is more to it than merely enduring. It's one thing to stand grim-faced, tightfisted, and staring at God with anger, saying, "How DARE YOU! What right do You have?" or "Look at what I've done for You! And look at what I get in return!" That's one kind of perseverance. But there's another kind. The kind that stands with open hands and open arms, that looks into the face of God and replies, "I submit myself to You. I'm trying hard to hear what You're saying. I wholly and completely admit my dependence. I've run out of answers. I'm waiting."

Faith is like lighting the torch that passes from one person to the next. You can't light the torch of another if yours isn't burning.

You may be going through a trial so overwhelming that it's borderline unbearable. You want to see the end of the tunnel. Which is only natural, because once we see that little speck of light, we feel we can make it through to the finish. But God's tunnels are often twisting, too complex and dark for us to see the light for many days. In such settings He says, "In that dark, twisting, seemingly endless period of time, trust Me. Stop running scared! Stop fearing!"

Did you know that you operate at your poorest when you are scared? A little fear is good for us when danger is present, but a lot of it is demoralizing. It takes away the hope, the dream, the vision, the possibility of overcoming. Jesus speaks with a gentle voice and says, "Don't be afraid! If I can't meet your need, what kind of a Savior would I be? Trust Me. Quietly trust Me."

Fears lurk in the shadows of every area of life. Perhaps you've suddenly discovered that an unexpected addition to your family is on the way. Don't be afraid. God can enable you to handle four kids just like He helped you handle three. You may be uncertain where your job is leading. The future may look threatening. You are uneasy about what's around the corner. Or perhaps you are afraid of what the doctor's exam might reveal. Jesus says, "Stop being afraid. Trust Me!"

One of the Greek terms for *tribulation* in the New Testament refers to "pressure . . . like being crushed under a big boulder." This is a description of pain, of enduring strain. It's an illustration of the crush of our times. There's a certain kind of pressure that comes with unemployment. There's another kind of pressure that comes with the threat of losing your home. There's a pressure that comes from calamity or a wayward child or a runaway mate. There's certainly pressure that comes with having too much to do and not having enough time to get it all done, a pressure that accompanies sleepless nights and the press of tomorrow's demanding responsibilities.

Annie Johnson Flint wrote:

Pressed out of measure and pressed to all length;
Pressed so intently it seems beyond strength.
Pressed in body and pressed in soul;
Pressed in the mind till the dark surges roll;
Pressure by foes, pressure by friends;
Pressure on pressure, till life nearly ends.
Pressed into loving the staff and the rod;
Pressed into knowing no helper but God. [3]

Jesus Christ stands at the door. He holds out His hands that are scarred. His feet are pierced, and He bears in His body the marks of death. He says, "I know the pressure you are under. I understand the strain. I know the unfair abuse. But let me offer you some encouragement. Don't be afraid. Look at life through My eyes! Stop letting life intimidate you! Stop running scared. Trust Me!"

Our English word *worry* is from the German *worgen*, which in that tongue means "to strangle."

The common response to trials is resistance, if not outright resentment. How much better that we open the doors of our hearts and welcome the God-ordained trials as honored guests for the good they do in our lives.

Anybody can accept a reward graciously, and many people can even take their punishment patiently when they have done something wrong. But how many people are equipped to handle mistreatment after they've done right? Only Christians are equipped to do that.

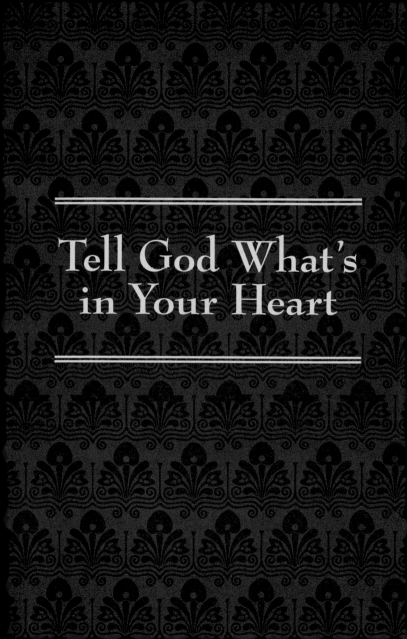

Tell God What's in Your Heart

Tell God What's in Your Heart

Does God care about the number of hairs in your scalp? Does He care if a sparrow falls? Yes, His Word assures us He does. Then be assured of this: He's a specialist in the things that worry you down inside. The things you dread tomorrow or this coming week. The things that make you wonder, "How can I get this together?" God's reassurance to you is "Look, that's what I specialize in. I can take that situation you've built into a mountain, and I can bore a tunnel through it in a matter of seconds. Bring all of it to Me. Ask Me to take charge. You don't have because you don't ask."

I wonder how many wonderful gifts are left wrapped in heaven because they were never unwrapped on earth. They just remain there, unasked for. James wrote plainly, "You do not have because you do not ask" (James 4:2). In other words, if we would ask more, we would have more.

But what about the times when we do ask? Sometimes the answer is yes, sometimes it's no, and many times it's wait.

Let's consider the two major ingredients in most prayerful requests. The first is what I call the petition itself: "Lord, I ask for this. Lord, I don't have transportation. I need something to drive, something that will get me from home to work. I ask You to provide an automobile that I can afford." That's a petition.

Or "Lord, I'm thirty-three years old and waiting. I don't have a mate. I feel I should not be single all my life. I ask You to provide the right mate—a partner for life. And I ask You to make it so clear that I don't make a mistake." That's a petition.

Now, the second major ingredient is the desire behind the petition—the reason I'm asking. Petition is the "what" of prayer and desire is the "why." One of the best ways to understand prayer is to consider the dynamics of the petition/desire issue. I think there are three ways that God can respond to our prayers.

Tell God all that is in your heart, as one unloads one's heart, its pleasures and its pains, to a dear friend.

FRANÇOIS FÉNELON

First, He can say yes to our petition but no to our desire. God can say yes to what we're asking for, but He can also say no to the motive behind it. And He sometimes does that when we've asked for the right thing with the wrong motive.

At other times God will say no to our request, but yes to our greater need. God is good to give us not what we request but what we really need. He may not answer as you request, but He does answer, meeting the need in another way.

Sometimes God answers "yes, yes." Yes you'll have the request, and yes you'll have the desire behind it. "It will honor Me. It's My will. It is for My glory. Yes, yes, in abundance." That's a great moment, when you ask for all the right reasons and God gives you a resounding yes. You get what you requested, and the reason you requested it is also honored.

But let's also consider the other times, the times when God says no—no to both our petition and our desire. What are some of the reasons for Him to answer a firm no? Well, unconfessed sin. An unclear conscience. Hypocrisy or pride. Selfishness. Perhaps a lack of faith. But, remember . . . He may say no simply because it isn't His will.

There are also times when God answers wait. Dr. Bing Hunter once wrote:

God's delay in giving answers seems to be a major way He encourages faith. Having seen that He is faithful following prayer over a week, you find it easier to trust Him for ten days. Seeing the answer to persistence after a month, strengthens me to wait in faith even longer for another month. The implications of this—no matter how many instant answers God may be pleased to give along the way—is that Christians will never arrive at a faith plateau where they trust God just enough.[4]

The wait forces us to trust Him. I think if I could gather all the needs of everyone who reads this book into one great response and I could ask each one, "Are you waiting for something right now, waiting for an answer to prayer?" I think more than likely every person would say yes. We are all waiting for an answer to prayer. God hasn't said no, but He hasn't said yes, either. He's said, "Wait." Do you know what that's doing in your Christian life? It's building muscles of faith.

God says, "I know what I'm doing. You can trust Me." And let me assure you. He is a good God, and you can trust Him whether He answers yes, no, or wait.

Some of you are going through trials right now that have dropped you on your knees. At the same time those trials are pulling you closer to the Lord than you've ever been in your life. That ought to bring rejoicing. You'll be more closely linked to Him.

When God says no, it is not necessarily discipline or rejection. It may simply be redirection.

Enduring Faith

Enduring Faith

We're very fickle in our faith, aren't we? We are inconsistent, ambivalent. We sing, "My faith looks up to Thee" . . . until the medicine stops working, until the lights go out, until the bill comes due and we don't have what it takes to pay it. Until our grades slip or our career takes a turn or we lose a mate. We have faith for a few days, but we can't stand it for a month or two. And if we lose our health . . . that's another story.

How do we learn consistent faith? We learn it one day at a time. We learn it through *endurance*. James wrote: "Consider it all joy, my brethren, when you encounter various trials, knowing that the testing of your faith produces endurance. And let endurance have its perfect result, so that you may be perfect and complete, lacking in nothing" (1:2–4). He wasn't talking about a will-o'-the-wisp faith that starts out like the 100-meter sprint and, quicker than you can think, is over. Anybody can handle that kind of faith. Anybody can take ten, fifteen, or twenty minutes of a test. But ten days or fifteen days? Or a year, or two or three? Well, that's another matter. That's the enduring faith James was talking about. Long-term faith is part of perfect trust.

Perfect trust results in perfect results. Which reminds me of a wheel that turns, makes a full cycle, and comes back to the same point every once in a while. That is how faith is built. God says to us, "Don't run! Don't escape! Don't give up! Let your faith run its course, that you might know how good I can be."

The writer of Hebrews also talked about endurance: "But My righteous one shall live by faith; and if he shrinks back, My soul has no pleasure in him" (Hebrews 10:38). Again I remind you, he was not talking about little short bursts of faith, but a regular habit of living by faith. It's a lifestyle faith designed for us today.

Now you may say, "I'm just not the type. I'm not called into the ministry. I'm not a preacher I'm a businessman. That faith stuff may be okay for you, but it's not for me." Or you may say, "You don't know my background. If you could read my track record, you wouldn't even waste your breath, because if there is any possible way to fail, I've done it." Stop! You misunderstand. If you think you've got to be a certain type of person to live by faith, you're sadly mistaken. Consider the list of examples of faith God highlighted for us in Hebrews 11.

In doing so, let's go back to that first excuse in light of these examples: "I'm not the type." Consider Noah. He was a farmer, but he went into the boat-building business for a period of 120 years. Then there is Abraham. He was a businessman raised by idolatrous parents. He was not a prophet. He was "just a businessman." And how about Sarah? She was a homemaker, plain and simple. She wasn't a prophetess or a woman preacher. She was a homemaker, but she was included in the inspired record as a woman of faith. There's also Joseph. He was a slave with a prison record, but then he became a prime minister. Moses was a shepherd who worked for his father-in-law out in the desert. He didn't do a thing that was spiritually significant for eighty years! And what about Rahab, the harlot? How can a woman with that kind of background be a woman of faith? Well, ask God; He is responsible for the record.

How do we learn consistent faith? We learn it one day at a time. We learn it through *endurance*.

Now let's consider the second excuse: "You don't know my background." Let's look again at Noah.

Noah got his name in lights because he built a barge that made it through the flood. But what people don't always remember is that shortly after the flood, Noah got drunk and was a shame to his children. And Abraham was a liar. He had a character weakness. He lied—and often at the expense of his dear wife. To save his own skin, he put her neck on the line. That's Abraham.

Sarah? She laughed when God told her she would have a baby at the age of ninety. (Wouldn't you?) And Jacob? You'd never want to do business with Jacob. He was a chiseler! He had this habit of deceiving. And it wasn't until God crippled him both in character and in physique that God got hold of him and made a prince out of him. Moses? He was a murderer. And he tried to hide the body in a shallow grave in Egypt.

You see, these people simply believed that God existed in the situation they were faced with, and they trusted Him rather than themselves. The result? God said, "That pleases Me." They were men and women just like you and me, which is the most encouraging part of all. We don't find golden haloes, or perfect backgrounds, or sinless lives; we just find people. People who failed, who struggled, who doubted, who experienced hard times and low times in which their faith was eclipsed with doubt. But their lives were basically characterized by faith.

Circumstances and Faith

Now let me clarify two things about faith as it relates to our circumstances. First of all, *the odds are always going to be overwhelming.* When you determine to trust God, the odds will always be against you. They will never be in your favor. Never. Otherwise, there's no need to trust. If you can work it out, that's not a test of faith. But if you can't handle it, then you've got the markings of a most exciting moment. Let's look at the odds for Noah. There had never been rainfall, and he built an ark. There had never been rain! But he believed that God would send rain. So he built the ark and got his family and the animals together. But remember, there had never been a drop of rain, and the odds were against there ever being rain. But Noah believed against the odds.

The second point I want to make is that *the outcome is not always pleasant*. Never believe that if you walk by faith, you've got the world by the tail. God never promised us a rose garden! Faith does not change my circumstances; faith changes me. Faith may not bring the tuition check when I need it, but faith will give me what it takes to hang on. Faith may not keep your husband from running away, but faith will give you the endurance it takes to hang in there if he does.

> Trusting God doesn't alter our circumstances. Perfect trust in Him changes us.

You see, when we talk about perfect trust, we're talking about what gives us roots, character, the stability to handle the hard times. Trusting God doesn't alter our circumstances. Perfect trust in Him changes us. It doesn't make life all rosy and beautiful and neat and lovely and financially secure and comfortable. But trust that is rooted in an abiding faith in God makes all that real in us—secure, relaxed, and calm against insuperable odds.

You know one of the most encouraging things about faith? *It pleases God.* In fact, "Without faith it is impossible to please Him" (Hebrews 11:6). That's why I want to encourage you: Walk by faith! Stop this plagued biting of nails and weariness of worry that you encourage within when the tests come. Relax! Learn to say, "Lord, this is Your battle. This is Your need that You've allowed me to trust You for. And I'm waiting for You to do it. I'm willing to wait as long as necessary for You to do the impossible."

When God sees this kind of faith, He smiles in return and responds, "I'm ready to support you. Give Me that need! Cast it on Me!" He stands ready to "support those whose heart is completely His" (2 Chronicles 16:9). These are the kind of people God is searching for: People who act in faith. People whose lives are being turned right side up through perfect trust.

Are you becoming one of those people?

We are never closer to the Lord, never more a recipient of His strength, than when trials come upon us.

Strength comes from
choosing to fully trust, pray,
and praise. Our circumstances
may not change, but in
the process we change.

God's Way
Is Right

God's Way Is Right

I s there something you are waiting for, something you are trusting God to do, to perform, to fulfill, and He hasn't done it yet? You are probably waiting longer than you thought you would have to wait. But that doesn't mean God's provision is canceled; it just means His promise is delayed. Our timetable is different from His, and on occasion He will say, "Wait." I repeat, the delay doesn't mean He has canceled it; the delay simply means He's building our character through the process of waiting. Perfect trust is a character-building process.

God is bringing significant things to pass. While He doesn't reveal what they are, He remains in control. He takes full responsibility, and it is His plan for you to rest in His rulership and reign over you. It makes a tremendous difference in life when we realize that we are not sovereign over our lives, nor are we expected to be. God is. God alone. We need to come to a place where we resign ourselves to our sovereign God. And when we do embrace God's sovereignty, we find that confidence increases, insecurities fade, worries decrease, and calmness replaces striving.

On what basis would we allow God to be in charge of our lives? Recently, I thought through a rather carefully worded résumé for someone who has the right to rule life: one who is absolutely powerful, infinitely wise, and completely objective. I think you'll find that only God qualifies. What makes God qualified? Well, anyone who is sovereign must see the end as perfectly as the beginning, must have a clear and unbiased perspective at all times, and must never operate from prejudice. He must entertain no fears, possess no ignorance, have no needs, and experience no frustration, limitations, or restrictions. He must have no match or rival on earth or in heaven. He must always know what is best and pursue that goal consistently, never making a mistake. He must be invincible, immutable, omnipotent, and self-sufficient. His judgments must be unsearchable, His ways unfathomable, and His will unchangeable. He must be able to create rather than invent, direct rather than wish, control rather than suggest, guide rather than guess, fulfill rather than dream, and bring everything to a perfect conclusion rather than close His eyes and hope for the best.

When we do embrace God's sovereignty, we find that confidence increases, insecurities fade, worries decrease, and calmness replaces striving.

Do you know anybody who qualifies? Not a soul! That's why God alone has the right to be sovereign over our lives. Our all-wise, all-knowing God reigns in realms beyond our comprehension, to bring about a plan that is beyond our ability to hinder, alter, or stop. But what would His plan include? It includes all promotions and demotions, occupations and losses of occupations. It includes prosperity and adversity, tragedy and ecstasy, joy and sorrow, gain and loss. It envelops illness as well as good health, healing as well as disease, perilous times and comfortable times, safety and ease as well as disasters and calamities. It would include all handicaps, heartaches, helpless moments, disappointments, broken dreams, and lingering difficulties as well as significant accomplishments and amazing discoveries.

God alone qualifies. He alone is worthy of our worship and praise. Being sovereign, He is in charge of all life! The day we resign ourselves to that is the day we really begin to understand what it means to rest by faith in a living God through Jesus Christ. When I don't fathom why, He knows. When I haven't a clue as to when, He understands. And when I cannot imagine good coming from something, He brings it to pass.

God will be all in all. God will have His way. What seems frustrating and wrong and unfair is not the end of the story. It's just the end of a chapter. The book He is writing has many, many chapters. Augustine was correct—absolutely right—when he said, "We count on God's mercy for our past mistakes; we count on God's love for our present needs; but we count on God's sovereignty for the future."

Our all-wise, all-knowing God reigns in realms beyond our comprehension, to bring about a plan that is beyond our ability to hinder, alter, or stop.

We are not in the hands of blind fate! We are in the hands of God, whose purposes are very clearly set forth, and whose goals fit perfectly into His plan. Our all-wise, all-knowing God is in charge. He has all the answers. He is the originator, the enforcer, and the provider. To Him be the glory forever and ever.

As John Oxenham wrote centuries ago:

He writes in characters too grand

For our short sight to understand;

We catch but broken strokes, and try

To fathom all the mystery
Of withered hopes, of death, of life,
The endless war, the useless strife—
But there, with larger clearer sight,
We shall see this—His way was right,
His way was right.[5]

God alone is deserving of our perfect trust.

When our future is foggy or fuzzy,
the Lord is our only hope.

Paul had a thorn in the flesh, and he prayed three times for God to remove it. "No," said God, "I'm not taking it away." Finally Paul said, "I've learned to trust in You, Lord. I've learned to live with it." It was then God said, "My grace is sufficient for that thorn." He matched the color of the test with the color of grace.

As a result of God's mercy, we have become a people who are uniquely and exclusively cared for by God. The fact that we are the recipients of His mercy makes all the difference in the world as to how we respond to difficult times. He watches over us with enormous interest.

Scriptures to Steady Your Heart

Trust

- Trust in the LORD with all your heart, and do not lean on your own understanding. In all your ways acknowledge Him, and He will make your paths straight. (Proverbs 3:5–6)

- The LORD is my strength and my shield; my heart trusts in Him, and I am helped; therefore my heart exults, and with my song I shall thank Him. (Psalm 28:7)

Worry

- "Therefore I tell you, do not worry about your life, what you will eat or drink; or about your body, what you will wear. Is not life more than food, and the body more than clothes? Look at the birds of the air; they do not sow or reap or store away in barns, and yet your heavenly Father feeds them. Are you not much more valuable than they? Who of you by worrying add a single hour to your life?" (Matthew 6:25–27 NIV)

- Cast all your anxiety on him because he cares for you. (1 Peter 5:7 NIV)

- "O men of little faith. Do not be anxious then, saying, "What shall we eat?" or "What shall we drink?" or "What shall we wear?" For the Gentiles seek all these things; and

your heavenly Father knows that you need
them. But seek first his kingdom and his
righteousness; and all these things shall be
yours as well" (Matthew 6:31–33 RSV)

Strength

- What then shall we say to these things? If God is for us, who is against us? He who did not spare His own Son, but delivered Him over for us all, how will He not also with Him freely give us all things? (Romans 8:31–32)

- But in all these things we overwhelmingly conquer through Him who loved us. For I am convinced that neither death, nor life, nor angels, nor principalities, nor things present, nor things to come, nor powers, nor height, nor depth, nor any other created thing, will be able to separate us from the love of God, which is in Christ Jesus our Lord. (Romans 8:37–39)

Comfort

- Let me hear Your lovingkindness in the morning; for I trust in You; teach me the way in which I should walk; for to You I lift up my soul. (Psalm 143:8)

- Whoever dwells in the shelter of the Most High will rest in the shadow of the Almighty. I will say of the LORD, "He is my refuge and my fortress, my God, in whom I trust." (Psalm 91:1–2 NIV)

Hope

- When I am afraid, I will put my trust in You. In God, whose word I praise, in God I have put my trust; I shall not be afraid. What can mere man do to me? (Psalm 56:3–4)

Peace

- In peace I will both lie down and sleep, for You alone, O LORD, make me to dwell in safety. (Psalm 4:8)
- The steadfast of mind You will keep in perfect peace, because he trusts in You. (Isaiah 26:3)
- When a man's ways are pleasing to the LORD, He makes even his enemies to be at peace with him. (Proverbs 16:7)

NOTES

1. A. W. Tozer, *That Incredible Christian* (Camp Hill, PA: Christian Publications, 1955).

2. Andrew Murray, *Abiding in Christ* (New Kensington, PA: Whitaker House, 1979).

3. Annie Johnson Flint, quoted in John R. Rise, *Poems That Preach* (Murfreesboro, TN: Sword of the Lord Publishing, 1952).

4. Bing Hunter, *The God Who Hears* (Downers Grove, IL: InterVarsity Press, 1986).

5. John Oxenham, *Bees in Amber* (New York: American Tract Society, 1913).

CHARLES R. SWINDOLL has devoted his life to the clear, practical teaching and application of God's Word and His grace. A pastor at heart, Chuck has served as senior pastor to congregations in Texas, Massachusetts, and California. Since 1998, he has served as the senior pastor-teacher of Stonebriar Community Church in Frisco, Texas, but Chuck's listening audience extends far beyond a local church body. As a leading program in Christian broadcasting since 1979, *Insight for Living* airs in major Christian radio markets around the world, reaching people groups in languages they can understand. Chuck's extensive writing ministry has also served the body of Christ worldwide and his leadership as president and now chancellor of Dallas Theological Seminary has helped prepare and equip a new generation for ministry. Chuck and Cynthia, his partner in life and ministry, have four grown children and ten grandchildren.